Presented to

Discover in this unique volume
the administrative highlights,
scientific achievements and
historical events
during terms of those who
held the nation's highest office,
relating two hundred years
of our country's history
through the lives of our Presidents.

from

Pageant of the Presidents

This limited edition of portraits of our Presidents, with vital information about each one's life, and his term as President, is offered by Realtors® as a nonprofit collection. By this means, they express their regard for the contribution these men have made to the pageant of our nation's history.

This Copy Of

"The Pageant of Presidents"

is No. 2803

of a limited edition

of

Five Thousand Copies

From The

Pageant of Presidents Committee

Signed hereby

Richard C. Hyer

Jerry F. Farrow

About the artist . . .

SAM J. PATRICK

By determination and experiment, Sam J. Patrick taught himself the craft of his choice. Born in Philadelphia of Russian immigrant parents, Mr. Patrick studied art in night classes at the Spring Garden Institute, while working in the steel mills and the Philadelphia Navy Yard. He moved to California and continued his studies at the Otis Art Institute before taking a position with a Los Angeles newspaper. This was the beginning of a 40-year career as a newspaper staff artist.

Mr. Patrick has collaborated with writers to create and produce internationally syndicated features. His work has appeared in more than 600 newspapers with a total circulation numbering in the millions. His portraits of presidents series is a culmination of years of experimentation. Mr. Patrick is the master of a new medium and technique, that of the wax color pencil, which provides an enormous vitality and detail in the portraiture. His most cherished award is the George Washington honor medal from the Freedoms Foundation at Valley Forge.

GEORGE WASHINGTON

GEORGE WASHINGTON
1st President

Born:
Feb. 22, 1732
Birthplace:
Pope's Creek, Westmoreland County, Va.
College attended:
None
Religious denomination:
Episcopalian
Ancestry:
English
Occupation:
Surveyor, planter
Date and place of marriage:
Jan. 6, 1759, Kent County, Va.
Age at marriage:
26 years, 318 days
Years married:
40 years, 342 days
Political party:
Federalist
State represented:
Virginia
Term of office:
Apr. 30, 1789—Mar. 3, 1797
Term served:
7 years, 308 days
Administration:
1st, 2nd
Congresses:
1st, 2nd, 3rd, 4th
Age at inauguration:
57 years, 67 days
Lived after term:
2 years, 285 days
Occupation after term:
Planter and General of the Army
Date of death:
Dec. 14, 1799
Age at death:
67 years, 295 days
Place of death:
Mount Vernon, Va.
Burial place:
Family vault, Mount Vernon, Va.

United States Population: 3,929,214 (1790)

Highlights of Administration: United States Bank founded . . . creation of federal judiciary, cabinet system . . . establishment of District of Columbia . . . states admitted: Vermont, Kentucky, Tennessee.

Scientific Achievement: 1792, gas lighting—William Murdock of Scotland . . . 1794, cotton gin—Eli Whitney of United States.

Historical Events: 1789, French Revolution following storming of Bastille . . . 1791, Bill of Rights became part of United States Constitution . . . 1792, United States Mint established by authority of Congress.

Washington was the only President who was inaugurated in two cities (New York City, April 30, 1789, and Philadelphia, Pa., March 4, 1793). He was the only President who did not live in Washington, D.C. and the first and only President unanimously elected, having received 69 of the 69 electoral votes cast.

He disapproved of swearing, rejected monarchy and borrowed money to go to his first inauguration. Washington's formal education ceased before he was 17. However, he did much studying on his own and although he lacked a college degree, five of the country's foremost colleges saw fit to confer honorary degrees upon him. During his two terms of office, Washington vetoed only two bills.

He was one of our richest Presidents and at his death his estate was valued at more than a half million dollars. The first town named for Washington was Forks of Tar River, N.C., which changed its name to Washington in 1775.

Being the first President, Washington established many "firsts." Included were the first whose mother was alive when he was inaugurated; to marry a widow; whose mother was a second wife; to have stepbrothers; to be depicted on a United States postage stamp; to refuse a third term; and the first to be born in Virginia.

JOHN ADAMS
2nd President

Born:
Oct. 30, 1735
Birthplace:
Braintree (now Quincy), Mass.
College attended:
Harvard College, Cambridge, Mass.
Date of graduation:
July 16, 1775, four-year course, Bachelor of Arts
Religion:
Unitarian
Ancestry:
English
Occupation:
Lawyer
Date and place of marriage:
Oct. 25, 1764, Weymouth, Mass.
Age at marriage:
28 years, 360 days
Years married:
54 years, 3 days
Political party:
Federalist
State represented:
Massachusetts
Term of office:
Mar. 4, 1797—Mar. 3, 1801
Term served:
4 years
Administration:
3rd
Congresses:
5th, 6th
Age at inauguration:
61 years, 125 days
Lived after term:
25 years, 122 days
Occupation after term:
Writer
Date of death:
July 4, 1826
Age at death:
90 years, 247 days
Place of death:
Quincy, Mass.
Burial place:
First Unitarian Church, Quincy, Mass.

UNITED STATES POPULATION: 4,883,209 (1797)

HIGHLIGHTS OF ADMINISTRATION: Creation of Navy Department . . . Alien and Sedition Acts.

SCIENTIFIC ACHIEVEMENT: None.

HISTORICAL EVENTS: None.

Adams was the first President born in Massachusetts and the only President whose son was inaugurated President. He was the second President whose mother was alive when he was inaugurated. Adams was the first President to reside in Washington, D.C. When he moved into the President's House on November 1, 1800, it was not completed and not a single apartment was finished. He was the first President to have children, blessed with three sons and two daughters. Adams was the first President to have a Justice of the Supreme Court administer the oath to him. He was sworn in on March 4, 1797, by Chief Justice Oliver Ellsworth.

Adams was the only President who was inaugurated at Philadelphia both as President and Vice President. On March 4, 1793, he was inaugurated as Vice President with George Washington as President, and on March 4, 1797, he was inaugurated President with Thomas Jefferson as his Vice President.

Adams was the first President who was defeated for reelection and he started the precedent of not attending the inauguration of his successor. Adams chose to absent himself rather than witness the success of his political rival, Thomas Jefferson. His wife was the first to live in the Executive Mansion.

JOHN ADAMS

THOMAS JEFFERSON

THOMAS JEFFERSON

3rd President

Born:
Apr. 13, 1743
Birthplace:
Shadwell, Goochland County, now Albemarle County, Va.
College attended:
College of William and Mary, Williamsburg, Va.
Date of graduation:
Apr. 25, 1762
Religion:
No specific denomination
Ancestry:
Welsh
Occupation:
Lawyer, writer
Date and place of marriage:
Jan. 1, 1772, Williamsburg, Va., at the Forest, the Wayles estate
Age at marriage:
28 years, 263 days
Years married:
10 years, 248 days
Political party:
Democratic-Republican
State represented:
Virginia
Term of office:
Mar. 4, 1801—Mar. 3, 1809
Term served:
8 years
Administration:
4th, 5th
Congresses:
7th, 8th, 9th, 10th
Age at inauguration:
57 years, 325 days
Lived after term:
17 years, 122 days
Occupation after term:
Retired
Date of death:
July 4, 1826
Age at death:
83 years, 82 days
Place of death:
Charlottesville, Va.
Burial place:
Charlottesville, Va.

United States Population: 5,485,528 (1801)

Highlights of Administration: Louisiana Purchase doubled United States territory . . . Lewis and Clark expedition . . . war declared with Tripoli . . . first national highway construction authorized . . . abolishment of slave trade . . . state admitted: Ohio.

Scientific Achievement: 1804, Locomotive—Richard Trevithick of England . . . 1807, Commercial steamship—Robert Fulton of United States.

Historical Events: Napoleon became emperor of France.

Jefferson was the second President born in Virginia and the second to marry a widow. He was the first widower inaugurated President and also the first inaugurated in Washington, D.C. He was the first President who had been a governor of a state and the first to have served in a cabinet. Jefferson was the first President whose parents had twins and the first elected by the House of Representatives. He was the first President who had served as Secretary of State.

One of his greatest achievements was the bill establishing religious freedom which was drawn up by him and enacted by the Legislature of Virginia in 1779. He was also a strong advocate of the decimal system of currency. Jefferson was the first and last Vice President to defeat a President and he held the first presidential review of military forces from his residence at the White House.

During his tenure of office, United States territory increased about 846,000 square miles, with the Louisiana Purchase, practically doubling the area of the United States. The inscription on Jefferson's epitaph, which he wrote and which is placed over his grave reads, "Here was buried Thomas Jefferson, author of the Declaration of American Independence, of the statute of Virginia for religious freedom and father of the University of Virginia."

THOMAS JEFFERSON

JAMES MADISON

JAMES MADISON

4th President

Born:
Mar. 16, 1751
Birthplace:
Port Conway, Va.
College attended:
Princeton University, Princeton, N.J.
Date of graduation:
Sept. 25, 1771, Bachelor of Arts
Religion:
Episcopalian
Ancestry:
English
Occupation:
Lawyer
Date and place of marriage:
Sept. 15, 1794, Harewood, Jefferson County, Va.
Age at marriage:
43 years, 183 days
Years married:
41 years, 286 days
Political party:
Democratic-Republican
State represented:
Virginia
Term of office:
Mar. 4, 1809—Mar. 3, 1817
Term served:
8 years
Administration:
6th, 7th
Congresses:
11th, 12th, 13th, 14th
Age at inauguration:
57 years, 353 days
Lived after term:
19 years, 116 days
Occupation after term:
Retired
Date of death:
June 28, 1836
Age at death:
85 years, 104 days
Place of death:
Montpelier, Va.
Burial place:
Family plot, Montpelier, Va.

UNITED STATES POPULATION: 7,030,647 (1809)

HIGHLIGHTS OF ADMINISTRATION: Declaration of war against Great Britain, 1812 . . . scope of Federal power defined by Chief Justice Marshall . . . Harrison defeated Indian attacks at Tippecanoe . . . states admitted: Indiana, Louisiana.

SCIENTIFIC ACHIEVEMENT: None.

HISTORICAL EVENTS: 1814, War of 1812 ended by Treaty of Ghent (on paper).

Madison was the third President born in Virginia and the third whose mother was alive when he was inaugurated. He was also the third President to marry a widow and the first President who had been a Congressman. Madison was the first President regularly to wear trousers instead of knee breeches and the last surviving signer of the Constitution. He was the first President to face enemy gunfire while in office and the first and only President to exercise actively his authority as Commander-in-Chief.

He was the only President whose administration suffered the death of two Vice Presidents. During Madison's term of office, Mordecai Manuel Noah, a Jew, was appointed United States Consul with diplomatic powers to Tunis. He was the first Jewish diplomatic representative of the United States.

It was in 1811, during Madison's administration, that the "Conscience Fund" was started by an unknown person who sent an anonymous letter containing five dollars, since he had, he claimed, defrauded the government of that sum. For statistical and accounting purposes, such funds are listed by the government as "miscellaneous receipts."

JAMES MONROE

5th President

Born:
Apr. 28, 1758
Birthplace:
Westmoreland County, Va.
College attended:
College of William and Mary, Williamsburg, Va.
Date of graduation:
1776
Religion:
Episcopalian
Ancestry:
Scotch
Occupation:
Lawyer
Date and place of marriage:
Feb. 16, 1786, New York, N.Y.
Age at marriage:
27 years, 294 days
Years married:
44 years, 219 days
Political party:
Democratic-Republican
State represented:
Virginia
Term of office:
Mar. 4, 1817—Mar. 3, 1825
Term served:
8 years
Administration:
8th, 9th
Congresses:
15th, 16th, 17th, 18th
Age at inauguration:
58 years, 310 days
Lived after term:
6 years, 122 days
Occupation after term:
Writer
Date of death:
July 4, 1831
Age at death:
73 years, 67 days
Place of death:
New York, N.Y.
Burial place:
Hollywood Cemetery, Richmond, Va.

UNITED STATES POPULATION: 8,898,892 (1817)

HIGHLIGHTS OF ADMINISTRATION: Purchase of Florida from Spain . . . panic of 1819 . . . 1820, Missouri Compromise . . . proclamation of Monroe Doctrine . . . states admitted: Mississippi, Illinois, Alabama, Maine, Missouri.

SCIENTIFIC ACHIEVEMENT: None.

HISTORICAL EVENTS: 1821, Death of Napoleon while in exile.

Monroe became the fourth President born in Virginia and the first President who was inaugurated on March 5 (March 4 was a Sunday). He was also the first President who had been a senator and the last of the Virginia regime of Presidents (Washington, Jefferson, Madison, Monroe). Monroe was the first President whose daughter was married in the White House and the first to be inaugurated outdoors. The latter occasion, during his first inauguration, was the result of a controversy between the Senate and the House of Representatives over the distribution of seats. He rode to the Capitol accompanied by an escort of citizens.

Monroe became the first United States President to ride on a steamboat, the Savannah, on May 11, 1819. Africa honored Monroe by naming Liberia's capital city, Monrovia, in honor of him. This came about when Upper Guinea, West Africa, was acquired by the American Colonization Society, founded in 1817 for the purpose of colonizing free negroes from the United States. On August 15, 1824, the name of the country was changed to Liberia.

JAMES MONROE

JOHN QUINCY ADAMS

JOHN QUINCY ADAMS

6th President

Born:
July 11, 1767
Birthplace:
Braintree (now Quincy), Mass.
College attended:
Harvard College, Cambridge, Mass.
Date of graduation:
July 18, 1787, Bachelor of Arts
Religion:
Unitarian
Ancestry:
English
Occupation:
Lawyer
Date and place of marriage:
July 26, 1797 London, England
Age at marriage:
30 years, 15 days
Years married:
50 years, 212 days
Political party:
Democratic-Republican
State represented:
Massachusetts
Term of office:
Mar. 4, 1825—Mar. 3, 1829
Term served:
4 years
Administration:
10th
Congresses:
19th, 20th
Age at inauguration:
57 years, 236 days
Lived after term:
18 years, 356 days
Date of death:
Feb. 23, 1848
Age at death:
80 years, 227 days
Place of death:
Washington, D.C.
Burial place:
First Unitarian Church, Quincy, Mass.

UNITED STATES POPULATION: 11,252,237 (1825)

HIGHLIGHTS OF ADMINISTRATION: Opening of Erie Canal . . . Baltimore and Ohio Railroad construction begun.

SCIENTIFIC ACHIEVEMENT: None.

HISTORICAL EVENTS: None.

Adams was the first President whose father had signed the Declaration of Independence and the only President whose father had been President. He was the second President born in Massachusetts and the first who had been elected a member of Phi Beta Kappa. He was also the first to wear long trousers at his inauguration but it was said he was the President least interested in clothes, having worn the same hat for ten years.

Adams was the first President elected without receiving the plurality of the popular votes. He was the first and only President to have a son whose given name was George Washington. He was the first President whose son was married in the White House and the first President to be married abroad. When Adams took the oath of office as President, all former presidents, with the exception of Washington, were living.

Adams was the most badly defeated presidential candidate, excluding those nominated by minor parties. In the election of 1820, he received only one electoral vote, cast by a New Hampshire elector, whereas Monroe received 231 of the 232 electoral votes. After serving as President, Adams became a congressman, representing the Plymouth, Mass., district.

JOHN QUINCY ADAMS

ANDREW JACKSON

ANDREW JACKSON

7th President

Born:
Mar. 15, 1767
Birthplace:
Waxhaw, S.C.
College attended:
None
Religion:
Presbyterian
Ancestry:
Scotch-Irish
Occupation:
Soldier
Date and place of marriage:
Aug. 1791, Natchez, Miss.
(Jan. 17, 1794, Nashville, Tenn.—second ceremony)
Age at marriage:
24 years
Years married:
37 years
Political party:
Democratic
(Democratic-Republican)
State represented:
Tennessee
Term of office:
Mar. 4, 1829—Mar. 3, 1837
Term served:
8 years
Administration:
11th, 12th
Congresses:
21st, 22nd, 23rd, 24th
Age at inauguration:
61 years, 354 days
Lived after term:
8 years, 96 days
Date of death:
June 8, 1845
Age at death:
78 years, 85 days
Place of death:
Nashville, Tenn.
Burial place:
The Hermitage estate, Nashville, Tenn.

United States Population: 12,565,145 (1829)

Highlights of Administration: Texas declares independence . . . siege of the Alamo . . . beginning of railroad service . . . bank of United States charter vetoed . . . nullification of federal tariff by South Carolina countered . . . 1830, Oregon Trail . . . states admitted: Arkansas, Michigan.

Scientific Achievement: 1831, Electric generator—Michael Faraday of England . . . 1832, Electric telegraph—Samuel Morse of United States . . . 1834, Reaping machine—Cyrus McCormick of United States . . . 1835, Revolver—Samuel Colt of United States.

Historical Events: None.

Jackson was the first President born in a log cabin as well as the first born in South Carolina. He was the first born west of the Allegheny Mountains and the first to marry a woman who had been divorced. He was the first President to receive a plurality of popular votes but who failed to win the election (1824). Jackson was the second widower inaugurated President and the first presidential candidate named by a national nominating convention. He was the first President who was a resident of a state other than his native state.

He no doubt could have been elected for a third term, but as none of his predecessors had served more than two terms, he refused to be a candidate again. There are many estimates of the number of brawls and duels Jackson participated in with some sources maintaining the figure approaches 100.

The first attempt upon the life of a President was made on Jackson on January 30, 1835 in the rotunda of the Capitol. Jackson appointed the first Catholic Chief Justice of the Supreme Court and was the first President to have the Senate reject a presidential cabinet appointee. A surplus of $37 million in taxes accumulated during his tenure accumulated during his tenure and Congress voted to permit disbursement of all but $5 million to the states in proportion to their congressional representation.

ANDREW JACKSON

MARTIN VAN BUREN

MARTIN VAN BUREN

8th President

Born:
Dec. 5, 1782
Birthplace:
Kinderhook, N.Y.
College attended:
None
Religious denomination:
Dutch Reformed
Ancestry:
Dutch
Occupation:
Lawyer
Date and place of marriage:
Feb. 21, 1807 Catskill, N.Y.
Age at marriage:
24 years, 78 days
Years married:
11 years, 349 days
Political party:
Democratic
(Democratic-Republican)
State represented:
New York
Term of office:
Mar. 4, 1837—Mar. 3, 1841
Term served:
4 years
Administration:
13th
Congresses:
25th, 26th
Age at inauguration:
54 years, 89 days
Lived after term:
21 years, 142 days
Date of death:
July 24, 1862
Age at death:
79 years, 231 days
Place of death:
Kinderhook, N.Y.
Burial place:
Kinderhook Cemetery,
Kinderhook, N.Y.

UNITED STATES POPULATION: 15,843,452 (1837)

HIGHLIGHTS OF ADMINISTRATION: 1837, financial panic . . . ten-hour work day established . . . 1839, Abner Doubleday introduced baseball.

SCIENTIFIC ACHIEVEMENT: 1839, on paper photography—William H. Fox Falbot of England.

HISTORICAL EVENTS: 1837, Victoria crowned Queen of England.

Van Buren was the first President born in New York and the third widower inaugurated President. He was the first whose son died in a foreign country. He was the eighth President and eighth Vice President of the United States. He lived to see eight Presidents from eight different states succeed him. Van Buren was the last Vice President to be elected to succeed the President, under whom he served. He brought his four sons with him when he went to the White House in 1837. They were 20, 25, 27 and 30 years of age. Van Buren was the first President born a citizen of the United States and therefore never a British subject.

During the span of 14 weeks, Van Buren held three important positions. On December 20, 1828, he resigned the office of United States senator. Eleven days later, he was governor of New York State and 64 days after that, Van Buren was made Secretary of State under President Jackson, resigning the governorship on March 12 and assuming his new post on March 28.

Van Buren's inauguration was of great political importance since the Chief Justice of the United States Supreme Court, whose earlier appointments as Secretary of the Treasury and Associate Justice had not been confirmed by the Senate, swore in as President a man whose appointment as United States minister to Great Britain had likewise not been approved by the Senate. Van Buren's Vice President was the first Vice President elected by the Senate. Van Buren was the first of three presidents to serve in the same year (1841).

MARTIN VAN BUREN

WILLIAM HENRY HARRISON

WILLIAM HENRY HARRISON

9th President

Born:
Feb. 9, 1773
Birthplace:
Berkeley, Charles City County, Va.
College attended:
Hampden-Sydney College, Hampden-Sydney, Va.
Date of graduation:
None (attended college 1787-1790)
Religious denomination:
Episcopalian
Ancestry:
English
Occupation:
Soldier
Date and place of marriage:
Nov. 25, 1795, North Bend, Ohio
Age at marriage:
22 years, 289 days
Years married:
45 years, 130 days
Political party:
Whig
State represented:
Ohio
Term of office:
Mar. 4, 1841—Apr. 4, 1841
Term served:
32 days
Administration:
14th
Congresses:
27th
Age at inauguration:
68 days, 23 years
Lived after term:
Died in office
Date of death:
Apr. 4, 1841
Age at death:
68 years, 54 days
Place of death:
Washington, D.C.
Burial place:
William Henry Harrison Memorial State Park, North Bend, Ohio

United States Population: 17,732,715 (1841)

Highlights of Administration: Harrison died after serving one month in office.

Scientific Achievement: None.

Historical Events: None.

Harrison became the first President to die in office and the second resident of a state other than his native state. He was the fifth President born in Virginia and the last born before the American Revolution. Harrison was the second President whose father had been a signer of the Declaration of Independence. He was also the oldest President inaugurated, being 68 years and 23 days old when he took the oath of office.

Harrison was the first and only President who studied to become a doctor. He was regularly enrolled in the Medical Department of the University of Pennsylvania and completed 16 weeks of a 32-week course. He served the shortest term as President (March 4, 1841, to April 4, 1841). Harrison became the only President whose grandson (Benjamin Harrison) also became President. He was also the first to lie in state in the White House. Harrison was the first President-elect to arrive by railroad at Washington, D.C., for his inauguration.

His 8,578-word inaugural address, the longest on record, took one hour and 45 minutes and was delivered during cold and stormy weather by Harrison who refused to wear a hat or coat. He caught cold at the ceremonies and was prostrated by a chill on March 27, 1841, dying of pleurisy fever (pneumonia) eight days later.

WILLIAM HENRY HARRISON

JOHN TYLER

JOHN TYLER
10th President

Born:
Mar. 29, 1790
Birthplace:
Charles City County, Va.
College attended:
William and Mary, Williamsburg, Va.
Date of graduation:
July 4, 1807
Religion:
Episcopalian
Ancestry:
English
Occupation:
Lawyer
Dates and places of marriages:
Mar. 29, 1813, New Kent County, Va.
June 26, 1844, New York, N.Y.
Ages at marriage:
23 years/54 years, 89 days
Years married:
29 years, 165 days/17 years, 206 days
Political party:
Whig (originally Democratic)
State represented:
Virginia
Term of office:
Apr. 6, 1841—Mar. 3, 1845
(Succeeded upon Harrison's death.)
Term served:
3 years, 332 days
Administration:
14th
Congresses:
27th, 28th
Age at inauguration:
51 years, 8 days
Lived after term:
16 years, 320 days
Occupation:
Lawyer
Date of death:
Jan. 18, 1862
Age at death:
71 years, 295 days
Place of death:
Richmond, Va.
Burial place:
Hollywood Cemetery, Richmond, Va.

United States Population: 17,732,715 (1841)

Highlights of Administration: First news dispatch by telegraph . . . China treaty signed . . . annexation of Texas . . . state admitted: Florida.

Scientific Achievement: 1844, vulcanized rubber—Charles Goodyear of United States.

Historical Events: None.

Tyler was the sixth President born in Virginia and the first whose wife died while he was in office. He was the first Vice President elevated to the presidency through the death of a Chief Executive. He was elected as a Whig to the vice presidency and took office March 4, 1841. Upon the death of President Harrison, Tyler took the oath of office as President on April 6, 1841. Tyler was the first President to marry while in office. He remarried on June 26, 1844. He was also the first to marry on his birthday and the first whose father had been governor of a state (Virginia).

Tyler's entire cabinet resigned (with the exception of Secretary of State Daniel Webster) as the result of a bill which Tyler vetoed. The bill "to provide for the better collection, safekeeping and disbursement of public revenues by means of a corporation to be styled the First Corporation of the United States" was disapproved of by Tyler's cabinet. The first child born in the White House was Elizabeth Priscilla Tyler, daughter of Robert Tyler, and the granddaughter of President Tyler. The first legislation to pass over a President's veto occurred while Tyler was in office.

When former President Tyler died in 1862, the government made no announcement or proclamation of his death and no official notice of his demise was taken. However, in 1911, some 50 years after his death, Congress authorized a monument to Tyler's memory, and dedicated it in 1915.

JOHN TYLER

JAMES KNOX POLK

JAMES KNOX POLK
11th President

Born:
Nov. 2, 1795
Birthplace:
Near Pineville, Mecklenburg County, N.C.
College attended:
Universtiy of North Carolina, Chapel Hill, N.C.
Date of graduation:
June 4, 1818, Bachelor of Arts
Religion:
Presbyterian
Ancestry:
Scotch-Irish
Occupation:
Lawyer
Date and place of marriage:
Jan. 1, 1824, Murfreesboro, Tenn.
Age at marriage:
28 years, 60 days
Years married:
25 years, 165 days
Political party:
Democratic
State represented:
Tennessee
Term of office:
Mar. 4, 1845—Mar. 3, 1849
Term served:
4 years
Administration:
15th
Congresses:
29th, 30th
Age at inauguration:
49 years, 122 days
Lived after term:
103 days
Occupation after term:
Retired because of illness
Date of death:
June 15, 1849
Place of death:
Nashville, Tenn.
Burial place:
State Capitol Grounds, Nashville, Tenn.

United States Population: 20,181,683 (1845)

Highlights of Administration: Discovery of gold in California . . . settlement of Oregon boundary . . . Mexican War—acquisition of California, New Mexico, Arizona, parts of Nevada and Colorado . . . states admitted: Texas, Iowa and Wisconsin.

Scientific Achievement: 1846, sewing machine—Elias Howe of United States . . . 1846, rotary printing—Richard Hoe of United States.

Historical Events: None.

Polk was the first President born in North Carolina and the third elected from a state other than his native state. He was the fourth President whose mother was alive when he was inaugurated and the first who was survived by his mother. The first use of the telegraph in politics occurred on May 29, 1844, when news was flashed to Washington, D.C., from Baltimore, Md., that Polk had been nominated for the presidency on the Democratic ticket.

He became the first "dark horse" elected President after a stalemate existed between former President Van Buren and Lewis Cass. Polk was suggested as a compromise candidate and eventually he received all of the 266 votes cast. Polk was the first Speaker of the House of Representatives who became President.

Since President and Mrs. Polk had no children, the First Lady's interests and time were devoted to her husband. She was extremely grave, formal, dignified and devoutly religious. As a result of the latter, she banned dancing and the serving of alcoholic beverages in the White House. Although the social set did not approve of this, the First Lady's policy was greatly admired by the strict religious elements of the nation.

JAMES KNOX POLK

ZACHARY TAYLOR

ZACHARY TAYLOR
12th President

Born:
Nov. 24, 1784
Birthplace:
Montebello, Orange County, Va.
College attended:
None
Religion:
Episcopalian
Ancestry:
English
Occupation:
Soldier
Date and place of marriage:
June 21, 1810, near Louisville, Ky.
Age at marriage:
25 years, 209 days
Years married:
40 years, 18 days
Political party:
Whig
State represented:
Louisiana
Term of office:
Mar. 4, 1849—July 9, 1850
Term served:
1 year, 127 days
Administration:
16th
Congresses:
31st
Age at inauguration:
64 years, 100 days
Lived after term:
Died in office
Date of death:
July 9, 1850
Age at death:
65 years, 227 days
Place of death:
Washington, D.C.
Burial place:
Springfield, Ky.

UNITED STATES POPULATION: 22,630,654 (1849)

HIGHLIGHTS OF ADMINISTRATION: Hawaiian Islands treaty . . . Clay Compromise of 1850 . . . California slavery struggle.

SCIENTIFIC ACHIEVEMENT: 1849, safety pin—Walter Hunt of United States.

HISTORICAL EVENTS: 1847, first Negro republic in Africa-Liberia.

Taylor was the seventh President born in Virginia and the second to die in office. He also was the second to be inaugurated on March 5 (March 4 was a Sunday). Taylor was the fourth elected from a state other than his native state and the second President to die in the White House. He became the third born after the Revolutionary War and the first representing a state west of the Mississippi (Louisiana) although a native of Virginia.

Taylor unwittingly refused to accept the letter of nomination sent by the Whigs notifying him of his nomination for the presidency since it arrived "postage due." Taylor refused to accept all unpaid mail.

He was too busy soldiering to vote, never staying in one place long enough to qualify as a voter, and being in the army, had not voted for 40 years. He cast his first vote at the age of 62. Shortly after his inauguration, Taylor announced the first appointee to the newly-established Home Department, later changed to the Department of Interior.

Taylor's wife refused to appear at public functions since she was in ill health and also because she had traveled from one military post to another during her husband's military career and preferred to live a quiet, simple life.

ZACHARY TAYLOR

MILLARD FILLMORE

MILLARD FILLMORE

13th President

Born:
Jan. 7, 1800
Birthplace:
Summerhill, Cayuga County, N.Y.
College attended:
None
Religion:
Unitarian
Ancestry:
English
Occupation:
Lawyer
Dates and places of marriages:
Feb. 5, 1826, Moravia, N.Y.
Feb. 10, 1858, Albany, N.Y.
Ages at marriages:
26 years, 29 days/58 years, 34 days
Years married:
27 years, 53 days/16 years, 36 days
Political party:
Whig
State represented:
New York
Term of office:
July 10, 1850—Mar. 3, 1853
(Succeeded upon Taylor's death.)
Term served:
2 years, 236 days
Administration:
16th
Congresses:
31st, 32nd
Age at inauguration:
50 years, 184 days
Lived after term:
21 years, 4 days
Occupation after term:
Chancellor of University of Buffalo
Date of death:
Mar. 8, 1874
Age at death:
74 years, 60 days
Place of death:
Buffalo, N.Y.
Burial place:
Forest Lawn Cemetery,
Buffalo, N.Y.

United States Population: 23,630,638 (1850)

Highlights of Administration: Enactment of Fugitive Slave Law . . . Commodore Perry opens Japan to commerce . . . state admitted: California.

Scientific Achievement: 1851, refrigerating machine—John Gorrie of United States . . . 1852, elevator—Elisha G. Otis of United States.

Historical Events: 1851, Moby Dick published in New York City—one of first significant novels . . . 1852, Uncle Tom's Cabin, Harriet Beecher Stowe.

Fillmore was the second President born in New York and the second whose father was alive when he was inaugurated. He was the second to remarry, the fourth to marry a widow and the first to have a stepmother. Fillmore was the second Vice President to succeed to the presidency on the death of a President.

When Fillmore took office, according to reports, the White House had no books, not even a Bible. His wife, a former schoolteacher and a voracious reader, converted a large room on the second floor to a library. Mrs. Fillmore was an invalid when her husband succeeded to the Presidency. Her daughter, therefore, assumed the functions of First Lady.

MILLARD FILLMORE

FRANKLIN PIERCE

FRANKLIN PIERCE
14th President

Born:
Nov. 23, 1804
Birthplace:
Hillsborough, N.Y.
College attended:
Bowdoin College, Brunswick, Me.
Date of graduation:
Sept. 1, 1824, four-year course, Bachelor of Arts
Religion:
Episcopalian
Ancestry:
English
Occupation:
Lawyer
Date and place of marriage:
Nov. 10, 1834, Amherst, Mass.
Age at marriage:
29 years, 352 days
Years married:
29 years, 22 days
Political party:
Democratic
State represented:
New Hampshire
Term of office:
Mar. 4, 1853—Mar. 3, 1857
Term served:
4 years
Administration:
17th
Congresses:
33rd, 34th
Age at inauguration:
48 years, 101 days
Lived after term:
12 years, 28 days
Occupation after term:
Retired; traveled
Date of death:
Oct. 8, 1869
Age at death:
64 years, 319 days
Place of death:
Concord, N.H.
Burial place:
Old North Cemetery, Concord, N.H.

United States Population: 25,736,070 (1853)

Highlights of Administration: Gadsden Purchase—acquisition of border territory from Mexico . . . Missouri Compromise nullified by Kansas-Nebraska Act . . . formation of Republican Party.

Scientific Achievement: 1855, steel production—Henry Bessemer of England.

Historical Events: None.

Pierce was the first President born in New Hampshire and the first born in the nineteenth century (Nov. 23, 1804). He was the first who did not read his 3,319-word inaugural address but instead delivered it as an oration. Pierce was a "dark horse" and not considered as a candidate until the 35th ballot when Virginia cast 15 votes for him. On the 49th ballot, there was a sudden surge in his favor and he received 283 of the 289 votes cast, thereby winning the nomination. He carried 27 of 31 states and defeated Gen. Winfield Scott, the Whig party nominee. In taking the oath of office, Pierce availed himself of an option provided in the Constitution, being the only President to solemnly "affirm" instead of "swear."

His inaugural ball was canceled since Pierce was in mourning for his son who had been killed in a railroad accident. Mrs. Pierce did not attend her husband's inauguration. Pierce was the only President to retain the same cabinet for four years without any replacements, changes, resignations or vacancies due to illness or death. President and Mrs. Pierce's three children died before they had reached their teens. Her grief was so great that she always dressed in black while in the White House.

FRANKLIN PIERCE

JAMES BUCHANAN

JAMES BUCHANAN
15th President

Born:
Apr. 23, 1791
Birthplace:
Cove Gap, Pa.
College attended:
Dickinson College, Carlisle, Pa.
Date of graduation:
Sept. 27, 1809, two-year course
Religion:
Presbyterian
Ancestry:
Scotch-Irish
Occupation:
Lawyer
Marital status:
Bachelor
Political party:
Democratic
State represented:
Pennsylvania
Term of office:
Mar. 4, 1857—Mar. 3, 1861
Term served:
4 years
Administration:
18th
Congresses:
35th, 36th
Age at inauguration:
65 years, 315 days
Lived after term:
7 years, 89 days
Occupation after term:
Writing
Date of death:
June 1, 1868
Age at death:
77 years, 39 days
Place of death:
Lancaster, Pa.
Burial place:
Woodward Hill Cemetery, Lancaster, Pa.

United States Population: 29,036,649 (1857)

Highlights of Administration: Dred Scott decision—Missouri Compromise unconstitutional . . . completion of Atlantic cable . . . John Brown raided Harpers Ferry . . . Southern states secede from the union . . . organization of Confederate States . . . states admitted: Minnesota, Oregon, Kansas.

Scientific Achievement: 1858, oil well—Edwin T. Holmes of United States . . . 1859, internal combustion engine—Jean Joseph E. Lenoir of France . . . 1860, repeating rifle—O. F. Winchester of United States . . . 1861, machine gun—Richard J. Gatling of United States.

Historical Events: 1860, Pony Express mail service begun between Missouri and California . . . 1861, organization of Confederate States.

Buchanan was the first President born in Pennsylvania and the only to remain a bachelor. However, he was engaged to marry but his fiancee, while on a visit to Philadelphia, took an overdose of laudanum and died. The first Republican platform was adopted during Buchanan's administration. Since he was a bachelor, the daughter of his sister served as mistress of the White House during his administration.

JAMES BUCHANAN

ABRAHAM LINCOLN

ABRAHAM LINCOLN
16th President

Born:
Feb. 12, 1809
Birthplace:
Hodgenville, Hardin County (now Larue County), Ky.
College attended:
None
Religion:
No specific denomination
Ancestry:
English
Occupation:
Lawyer
Date and place of marriage:
Nov. 4, 1842, Springfield, Ill.
Age at marriage:
33 years, 265 days
Years married:
22 years, 162 days
Political party:
Republican
State represented:
Illinois
Term of office:
Mar. 4, 1861—Apr. 15, 1865
Term served:
4 years, 42 days
Administrations:
19th, 20th
Congresses:
37th, 38th, 39th
Age at inauguration:
52 years, 20 days
Lived after term:
Died in office
Date of death:
Apr. 15, 1865
Age at death:
56 years, 62 days
Place of death:
Washington, D.C.
Burial place:
Oak Ridge Cemetery, Springfield, Ill.

United States Population: 32,350,627 (1861)

Highlights of Administration: Secession of Virginia, Arkansas, North Carolina, Tennessee . . . attack of Fort Sumter—Civil War . . . Emancipation Proclamation issued . . . Morrill land-grant college act . . . states admitted: West Virginia, Nevada.

Scientific Achievement: 1862, dynamite—Alfred B. Nobel of Sweden.

Historical Events: 1861, beginning of Civil War with bombardment of Fort Sumter . . . 1863, American protest of Mexican occupation by French troops . . . 1863, signing of Emancipation Proclamation by President Lincoln . . . 1863, Thanksgiving Day declared national holiday . . . 1865, Civil War ended—Lee surrendered to Grant at Appomatox, Virginia.

Lincoln was the first President born in Kentucky and the fifth elected from a state other than his native state. He was also the first to be assassinated and the third to die in office. He was the first President born outside of the original 13 states. At the first Republican Party convention, Lincoln was defeated in the race for vice presidential nomination. Lincoln's native state ignored him and another favorite son as presidential candidates, casting its 12 electoral votes for John Bell of Tennessee.

The first presidential executive order to be numbered was Order No. 1, signed by Lincoln. It was not the first executive order issued by a President, but the first one in the files of the Department of State. The first of the national Thanksgiving Day proclamations was issued by Lincoln who also issued the first amnesty proclamation to citizens.

Lincoln was the first President to rest in state at the United States Capitol rotunda. His funeral procession took 12 days and stops were made along the railroad route between Washington, D.C. and Springfield, Illinois. His body was moved 17 times from the night he was carried from Ford's Theatre until it was finally laid to rest in a tomb in Springfield in 1901. His son, Robert Todd Lincoln, was at the scene of three presidential assassinations. Besides his father's, he was at the assassination scenes of Presidents Garfield and McKinley.

ABRAHAM LINCOLN

ANDREW JOHNSON

ANDREW JOHNSON

17th President

Born:
Dec. 29, 1808
Birthplace:
Raleigh, N.C.
College attended:
None
Religion:
No specific denomination
Ancestry:
English
Occupation:
Tailor, legislator
Date and place of marriage:
May 5, 1827, Greeneville, Tenn.
Age at marriage:
18 years, 127 days
Years married:
48 years, 87 days
Political party:
Democratic (elected Vice President on Republican ticket)
State represented:
Tennessee
Term of Office:
Apr. 15, 1865—Mar. 3, 1869 (Succeeded upon Lincoln's death.)
Term served:
3 years, 323 days
Administration:
20th
Congresses:
39th, 40th
Age at inauguration:
56 years, 107 days
Lived after term:
6 years, 149 days
Occupation after term:
U.S. senator
Date of death:
July 31, 1875
Age at death:
66 years, 214 days
Place of death:
Carter's Station, Tenn.
Burial place:
Andrew Johnson National Cemetery, Greeneville, Tenn.

UNITED STATES POPULATION: 35,700,678 (1865)

HIGHLIGHTS OF ADMINISTRATION: Reconstruction period . . . secessionists pardoned . . . Johnson impeached by House, acquitted by Senate . . . purchase of Alaska . . . state admitted: Nebraska.

SCIENTIFIC ACHIEVEMENT: 1867, typewriter—Christopher L. Sholes of United States.

HISTORICAL EVENTS: 1867, United States purchase of Alaska from Russia . . . 1867, Canada became self-governing dominion of the British Empire.

Johnson was the second President born in North Carolina and the sixth elected from a state other than his native state. He was married at a younger age than any other President and was the first whose early background was not military or legal. Johnson was the first and only President against whom impeachment proceedings were brought.

He never attended school and was scarcely able to read when he met his wife. He was about 17 when she taught him how to write. Johnson was the first President to receive the visit of a queen, Queen Emma of the Sandwich Islands (Hawaii) upon her arrival in New York City in 1866. He was the first President to become a senator after his term of office, being elected senator from Tennessee.

When he took his seat in the 44th Congress, he was one of 74 senators. Only 14 had taken part in his trial of 1868, 12 of whom had voted him "guilty," and two of them "not guilty." Johnson's wife was an invalid when he became President, and as a result, their daughters acted as White House hostesses.

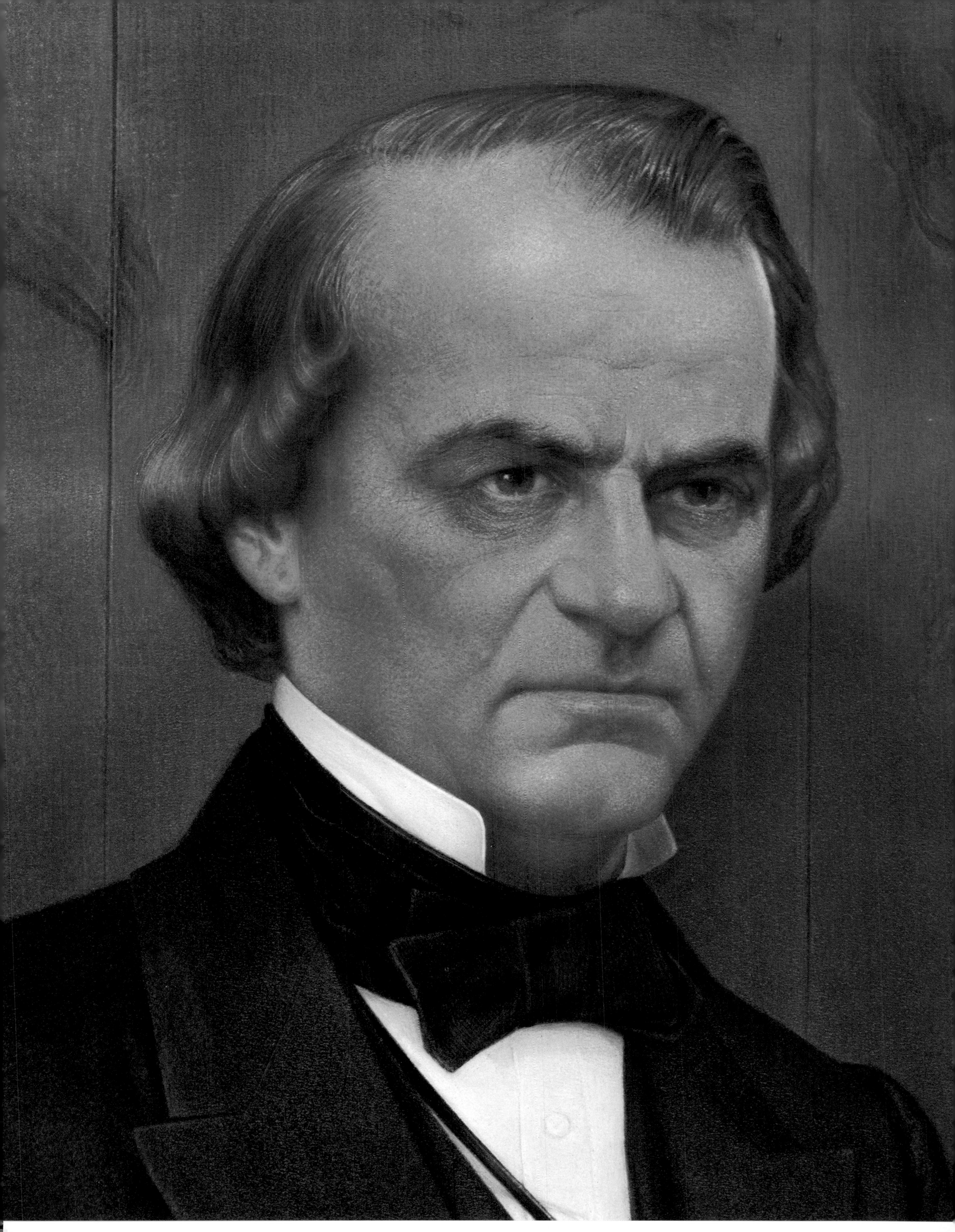

ULYSSES SIMPSON GRANT
18th President

Born:
Apr. 27, 1822 (Given name—Hiram Ulysses Grant)
Birthplace:
Point Pleasant, Ohio
College attended:
U.S. Military Academy, West Point, N.Y.
Date of graduation:
July 1, 1843, four-year course
Religion:
Methodist
Ancestry:
English, Scotch
Occupation:
Soldier
Date and place of marriage:
Aug. 22, 1848, St. Louis, Mo.
Age at marriage:
26 years, 117 days
Years married:
36 years, 335 days
Political party:
Republican
State represented:
Illinois
Term of office:
Mar. 4, 1869-Mar. 3, 1877
Term served:
8 years
Administration:
21st, 22nd
Congresses:
41st, 42nd, 43rd, 44th
Age at inauguration:
46 years, 311 days
Lived after term:
8 years, 141 days
Occupation after term:
Traveling and writing
Date of death:
July 23, 1885
Age at death:
63 years, 87 days
Place of death:
Mount McGregor, N.Y.
Burial place:
Grant's Tomb, New York, N.Y.

UNITED STATES POPULATION: 39,050,729 (1869)

HIGHLIGHTS OF ADMINISTRATION: Creation of Department of Justice . . . 15th Amendment—right to vote . . . administrative scandals . . . 1873, financial panic . . . state admitted: Colorado.

SCIENTIFIC ACHIEVEMENT: 1876, telephone—Alexander Graham Bell of United States.

HISTORICAL EVENTS: 1869, America's first transcontinental railroad joined at Promontory, Utah . . . 1870, beginning of Franco-Prussian War . . . 1871, France surrendered ending Franco-Prussian War . . . 1871, meeting of Stanley and Livingstone in Central Africa . . . 1876, Little Big Horn, Custer's last stand.

Grant was the first President born in Ohio and the seventh elected from a state other than his native state. He was the only President whose parents were both alive when he was inaugurated. Ulysses Simpson Grant was given the name Hiram Ulysses Grant when he was born. He transposed it to Ulysses Hiram Grant. When he applied for appointment to West Point, the congressman made an error and listed Grant as Ulysses Simpson Grant. Grant accepted the accidental change in his name. A letter by Grant, dictating the terms for the surrender of Fort Donelson, Tenn., earned him the nickname "Unconditional Surrender" Grant.

He suffered great financial reverses after his term of office and was almost destitute. To relieve this situation, Congress passed legislation restoring former President Grant to his old military status as general. One of the best-paying books of its time and still high on the all-time list is President Grant's "Memoirs." Royalties amounted to $500,000 but he never saw his book in type as he died four days after he had completed the manuscript. The first reigning king to visit the United States, David Kalakaua, King of the Sandwich Islands (Hawaii) was received by Grant in the White House in 1874.

ULYSSES SIMPSON GRANT

RUTHERFORD BIRCHARD HAYES

RUTHERFORD BIRCHARD HAYES

19th President

Born:
Oct. 4, 1822
Birthplace:
Delaware, Ohio
College attended:
Kenyon College, Gambier, Ohio
Date of graduation:
Aug. 3, 1842, Bachelor of Arts
Religion:
Attended Methodist Church
Ancestry:
Scotch
Occupation:
Lawyer
Date and place of marriage:
Dec. 30, 1852, Cincinnati, Ohio
Age at marriage:
30 years, 87 days
Years married:
40 years, 18 days
Political party:
Republican
State represented:
Ohio
Term of office:
Mar. 4, 1877-Mar. 3, 1881
Term served:
4 years
Administration:
23rd
Congresses:
45th, 46th
Age at inauguration:
54 years, 151 days
Lived after term:
11 years, 319 days
Occupation after term:
Philanthropic activities
Date of death:
Jan. 17, 1893
Age at death:
70 years, 105 days
Place of death:
Fremont, Ohio
Burial place:
Spiegel Grove State Park, Fremont, Ohio

UNITED STATES POPULATION: 47,140,727 (1877)

HIGHLIGHTS OF ADMINISTRATION: Bland-Allison Act, limited coinage of silver . . . federal troop withdrawal from South . . . 1877, railroad strikes.

SCIENTIFIC ACHIEVEMENTS: 1878, half-tone engraving process—Frederick E. Ives of United States . . . 1878, phonograph—Thomas A. Edison of United States . . . 1879, electric lamp—Thomas A. Edison of United States . . . 1879, cash register—James Ritty of United States.

HISTORICAL EVENTS: 1879, demonstration by Thomas A. Edison of first incandescent light bulb.

Hayes was the second President born in Ohio. He was the first sworn in on March 3 and the third inaugurated on March 5. Because it was the most disputed election in history, Hayes took the oath of office privately in the White House, the first time that a president-elect had taken the oath in the White House. No inaugural parade or ball was held. President Hayes and his wife celebrated their silver wedding anniversary in the White House. He became the first President to visit the West Coast, arriving in San Francisco on Sept. 8, 1880.

Both Hayes and his wife were total abstainers. As a result, his wife, Lucy, acquired the nickname of "Lemonade Lucy" because of her habit of serving lemonade and soft drinks instead of liquor at the White House.

RUTHERFORD BIRCHARD HAYES

JAMES ABRAM GARFIELD

JAMES ABRAM GARFIELD
20th President

Born:
Nov. 19, 1831
Birthplace:
Orange, Ohio
College attended:
Williams College,
Williamstown, Mass.
Date of graduation:
Aug. 6, 1856, four-year course
Religious denomination:
Disciples of Christ
Ancestry:
English
Occupation:
Teacher
Date and place of marriage:
Nov. 11, 1858, Hiram, Ohio
Age at marriage:
26 years, 357 days
Years married:
22 years, 312 days
Political party:
Republican
State represented:
Ohio
Term of office:
Mar. 4, 1881-Sept. 19, 1881
Term served:
199 days
Administration:
24th
Congresses:
47th
Age at inauguration:
49 years, 105 days
Lived after term:
Died in office
Date of death:
Sept. 19, 1881
Age at death:
49 years, 304 days
Place of death:
Elberon, N.J.
Burial place:
Lake View Cemetery,
Cleveland, Ohio

UNITED STATES POPULATION: 51,541,575 (1881)

HIGHLIGHTS OF ADMINISTRATION: Garfield served less than five months.

SCIENTIFIC ACHIEVEMENT: None.

HISTORICAL EVENTS: 1881, American Red Cross organized under leadership of Clara Barton.

Garfield was the third President born in Ohio and the first whose mother was present at his inauguration. He was the fourth President to die in office, the second to be assassinated. Garfield was the first to review an inaugural parade from a stand in front of the White House, the second to be survived by his mother and the first left-handed President.

Garfield studied Latin and Greek at Williams College and took up German as an elective, which proved helpful, as Garfield used the language in campaigning. A plurality of about one-tenth of one percent of the popular vote enabled Garfield to become President.

Garfield also qualified for three federal positions at the same time. He was a congressman from Ohio and while serving in the House of Representatives in 1880, was elected by the legislature of Ohio to serve in the United States Senate for the term beginning March 4, 1881. However, on Nov. 2, 1880, Garfield was elected President. On that date, he was president-elect, senator-elect and a member of the House of Representatives. The first act of Garfield after his inauguration was to kiss his mother who was the first mother of a President to live at the White House.

CHESTER ALAN ARTHUR

21st President

Born:
Oct. 5, 1830
Birthplace:
Fairfield, Vt.
College attended:
Union College, Schenectady, N.Y.
Date of graduation:
July 1848
Religion:
Episcopalian
Ancestry:
Scotch-Irish
Occupation:
Lawyer
Date and place of marriage:
Oct. 25, 1859, New York, N.Y.
Age at marriage:
29 years, 20 days
Years married:
20 years, 79 days
Political party:
Republican
State represented:
New York
Term of office:
Sept. 20, 1881—Mar. 3, 1885
(Succeeded upon Garfield's death.)
Term served:
3 years, 166 days
Administration:
24th
Congresses:
47th, 48th
Age at inauguration:
50 years, 350 days
Lived after term:
1 year, 260 days
Occupation after term:
Lawyer
Date of death:
Nov. 18, 1886
Age at death:
56 years, 44 days
Place of death:
New York, N.Y.
Burial place:
Rural Cemetery, Albany, N.Y.

United States Population: 51,541,575 (1881)

Highlights of Administration: Organization of Civil Service system . . . Nicaraguan treaty for canal construction . . . Chinese Exclusion Act—restricted immigration . . . territorial government established in Alaska . . . new protective tariff enacted.

Scientific Achievement: 1884, modern bicycle—Stanley of England . . . 1885, gasoline car—Karl Benz of Germany.

Historical Events: None.

Arthur was the first President born in Vermont, the eighth elected from a state other than his native state and the fourth widower inaugurated President. In 1881, for the second time in American history there were three Presidents in one year—Hayes, Garfield and Arthur.

Arthur took his oath of office at his New York City residence early on the morning of Sept. 20, 1881. Two days later the oath was repeated in the Vice President's room at the Capitol where it was administered in the presence of former Presidents Hayes and Grant.

Since Arthur's wife died before he succeeded to the presidency, and his only daughter was only ten years of age, the duties of mistress of the White House were assumed by his sister.

CHESTER ALAN ARTHUR

GROVER CLEVELAND

GROVER CLEVELAND

22nd and 24th President

Born:
Mar. 18, 1837 (Given name Stephen Grover Cleveland)
Birthplace:
Caldwell, N.J.
College attended:
None
Religion:
Presbyterian
Ancestry:
English-Irish
Occupation:
Lawyer, sheriff
Date and place of marriage:
June 2, 1886, Washington, D.C.
Age at marriage:
49 years, 76 days
Years married:
22 years, 22 days
Political party:
Democratic
State represented:
New York
Term of office:
(First Term): Mar. 4, 1885-Mar. 3, 1889. (Second Term): Mar. 4, 1893-Mar. 3, 1897
Terms served:
4 years each
Administrations:
25th, 27th
Congresses:
49th, 50th, 53rd, 54th
Age at inauguration:
(First Term): 47 years, 351 days
(Second Term): 55 years, 351 days
Lived after second term:
11 years, 112 days
Date of death:
June 24, 1908
Age at death:
71 years, 98 days
Place of death:
Princeton, N.J.
Burial place:
Princeton, N.J.

United States Population: 56,658,347 (1885)
66,970,496 (1893)

Highlights of Administration: Approval of Presidential Succession Act . . . appointment of first interstate Commerce Commission . . . organization of American Federation of Labor . . . repeal of Sherman Silver Purchase Act . . . Hawaii becomes a republic . . . beginning of Cuban revolt . . . pullman strikers meet federal troops . . . state admitted: Utah.

Scientific Achievement: 1887, automobile—Gottlieb Daimler of Germany . . . 1888, electric (A.C.) motor—Nikola Tesla of United States . . . 1888, Kodak camera—George Eastman of United States . . . 1894, wireless telegraph—Guglielmo Marconi of Italy . . . 1895, X-ray—Wilhelm Roentgen of Germany . . . 1895, motion pictures—Auguste Marie Louis Nicolas Lumiere and Louis Jean Lumiere of France.

Historical Events: 1885, U.S. Marines land in Panama . . . 1886, Statue of Liberty dedicated at Bedloe's Island . . . 1896, renewal of Olympic Games.

Cleveland was the first and only President born in New Jersey, the only President married in the White House, the ninth elected from a state other than his native state and the seventh whose mother was alive when he was inaugurated. Cleveland was the only President who was defeated for reelection and later reelected, thus serving two non-consecutive terms. He was the first President elected after the Civil War who did not take part in the war.

He was originally named Stephen Grover Cleveland, but dropped his first name in his youth. Instead of delegating disagreeable tasks, such as hangings, to others, Cleveland personally carried out the duties of two hangings while a sheriff in Buffalo, N.Y.

Cleveland received the plurality vote three times as a presidential candidate but won election only twice since Harrison won the electoral vote even though Cleveland defeated him by a popular vote of about 100,000.

The first child of a President to be born in the White House was the second child of President and Mrs. Cleveland.

GROVER CLEVELAND

BENJAMIN HARRISON

BENJAMIN HARRISON

23rd President

Born:
Aug. 20, 1883
Birthplace:
North Bend, Ohio
College attended:
Miami University, Oxford, Ohio
Date of graduation:
June 24, 1852, Bachelor of Arts
Religious denomination:
Presbyterian
Ancestry:
English
Occupation:
Lawyer
Dates and places of marriages:
Oct. 20, 1853
Apr. 6, 1896, New York, N.Y.
Ages at marriage:
20 years, 61 days/62 years, 229 days
Years married:
39 years, 5 days/4 years, 341 days
Political party:
Republican
State represented:
Indiana
Term of office:
Mar. 4, 1889-Mar. 3, 1893
Term served:
4 years
Administration:
26th
Congresses:
51st, 52nd
Age at inauguration:
55 years, 196 days
Lived after term:
8 years, 9 days
Occupation after term:
Lawyer, teacher
Date of death:
Mar. 13, 1901
Age at death:
67 years, 205 days
Place of death:
Indianapolis, Ind.
Burial place:
Crown Hill Cemetery, Indianapolis, Ind.

United States Population: 61,775,121 (1889)

Highlights of Administration: Sherman Anti-trust Act passed . . . Oklahoma opened to settlers . . . passage of Sherman Silver Purchase Act . . . states admitted: North Dakota, South Dakota, Montana, Washington, Idaho, Wyoming.

Scientific Achievement: 1891, zipper—Whitcomb L. Judson of United States.

Historical Events: None.

Harrison was the fourth President born in Ohio and the tenth President elected from a state other than his native state. He was the third President to remarry and the fifth to marry a widow. He was the second whose wife died while he was in office. He was the only grandson of a President to become President (William Henry Harrison, our ninth President). He was the only President preceded and succeeded by the same man and the only President who had two secretaries in his cabinet with the same last name (John Foster, Secretary of State, and Charles Foster, Secretary of the Treasury).

The first Congress to appropriate a billion dollars was in session during Harrison's administration. Harrison's second wife bore a daughter to her husband which was younger than Harrison's four grandchildren. His second wife was a niece of the President's first wife. She lived at the White House for two years taking charge of the social functions as Harrison's first wife had become an invalid. The President's second wife married him after the completion of his term of office.

BENJAMIN HARRISON

WILLIAM MCKINLEY

WILLIAM MCKINLEY
25th President

Born:
Jan. 29, 1843
Birthplace:
Niles, Ohio
College attended:
Allegheny College, Meadville, Pa.
Date of graduation:
Left before graduation
Religion:
Methodist
Ancestry:
Scotch-Irish
Occupation:
Lawyer
Date and place of marriage:
Jan. 25, 1871, Canton, Ohio
Age at marriage:
27 years, 361 days
Years married:
30 years, 232 days
Political party:
Republican
State represented:
Ohio
Term of office:
Mar. 4, 1897-Sept. 14, 1901
Term served:
4 years, 194 days
Administration:
28th, 29th
Congresses:
55th, 56th, 57th
Age at inauguration:
54 years, 34 days
Lived after term:
Died in office
Date of death:
Sept. 14, 1901
Age at death:
58 years, 228 days
Place of death:
Buffalo, N.Y.
Burial place:
Adjacent to Westlawn Cemetery, Canton, Ohio

UNITED STATES POPULATION: 72,189,240 (1897)

HIGHLIGHTS OF ADMINISTRATION: Hawaii annexed by United States . . . eruption of Spanish-American War . . . acquisition of Philippines, Guam, Puerto Rico . . . United States aids in suppressing Boxer Rebellion in China . . . initiation of new protective tariffs.

SCIENTIFIC ACHIEVEMENT: 1900, submarine—J. P. Holland of United States . . . 1900, caterpillar tractor—Benjamin Holt of United States.

HISTORICAL EVENTS: 1898, United States battleship Maine sunk in Havana harbor . . . 1898, United States declared war against Spain.

McKinley was the fifth President born in Ohio and the fifth to die in office. He was the third to be assassinated and the second Ohio-born President to be assassinated. He was also the fifth Ohio-born President elected within 28 years.

McKinley was the first to use the telephone for campaign purposes. In 1896 he telephoned 38 of his campaign managers in as many states from his residence in Canton, Ohio, on matters pertaining to his campaign.

Mrs. McKinley had been an invalid for many years before coming to the White House. She was an epileptic and had a seizure at the second inaugural ball. President McKinley was noted for his tender affection for and great devotion to his ailing wife.

WILLIAM MCKINLEY

THEODORE ROOSEVELT

THEODORE ROOSEVELT

26th President

Born:
Oct. 27, 1858
Birthplace:
New York, N.Y.
College attended:
Harvard University, Cambridge, Mass.
Date of graduation:
June 30, 1880, Bachelor of Arts
Religious denomination:
Dutch Reformed Church
Ancestry:
Dutch
Occupation:
Rancher, Lawyer, Political official
Dates and places of marriage:
Oct. 27, 1880, Brookline, Mass.
Dec. 2, 1886, London, England
Ages at marriage:
22 years/28 years, 36 days
Years married:
3 years, 110 days/32 years, 35 days
Political party:
Republican
State represented:
New York
Term of office:
Sept. 14, 1901—Mar. 3, 1909
(Succeeded upon McKinley's death.)
Term served:
7 years, 171 days
Administration:
29th, 30th
Congresses:
57th, 58th, 59th, 60th
Age at inauguration:
42 years, 322 days
Lived after term:
9 years, 309 days
Occupation after term:
Writer, big-game hunter, political leader
Date of death:
Jan. 6, 1919
Age at death:
60 years, 71 days
Place of death:
Oyster Bay, N.Y.
Burial place:
Young's Memorial, Oyster Bay, N.Y.

UNITED STATES POPULATION: 77,585,000 (1901)

HIGHLIGHTS OF ADMINISTRATION: Acquisition of Panama Canal Zone . . . creation of Department of Commerce and Labor . . . Russo-Japanese peace treaty signed . . . Pure Food and Drug Act passed . . . Monroe Doctrine corollary . . . financial panic of 1907 . . . state admitted: Oklahoma.

SCIENTIFIC ACHIEVEMENT: 1902, radium—Marie and Pierre Curie of France . . . 1903, airplane—Orville and Wilbur Wright of United States . . . 1905, Theory of Relativity—Albert Einstein of Germany . . . 1907, electric washing machine—Hurley Machine Co. of United States.

HISTORICAL EVENTS: 1901, first wireless from Europe . . . 1903, first successful airplane flight by Wright brothers . . . 1905, end of the Russo-Japanese war.

Roosevelt was the third President born in New York, the fourth to remarry and the second to be married on his birthday. He was the first President to win a Nobel peace prize and the youngest man to take the oath of office as Chief Executive. He was 42 years and 10 months when sworn in.

Feb. 14, 1884 was a day of tragedy for Roosevelt. On that day his mother died in New York City of typhoid fever and his first wife, Alice, died of Bright's disease. President Roosevelt was the first Chief Executive to ride in an automobile, taking the trip through Hartford, Conn. After his term of office, he again pioneered when he took a ride in an airplane at St. Louis, Mo.

The first man to hold the office of Secretary of Commerce and Labor was appointed by Roosevelt. He was the first to visit a foreign country during his term of office, traveling to Panama on the U.S.S. Louisiana. After visiting Panama, he went to Puerto Rico.

During the 1912 Presidential campaign, an assassination attempt was made on Roosevelt's life in Milwaukee, Wis. He was shot in the chest by a saloon keeper, who was later declared insane and committed to a state hospital. His would-be assassin was opposed to Roosevelt's attempt to capture a third term.

THEODORE ROOSEVELT

WILLIAM HOWARD TAFT

WILLIAM HOWARD TAFT

27th President

Born:
Sept. 15, 1857
Birthplace:
Cincinnati, Ohio
College attended:
Yale
Date of graduation:
June 27, 1878
Religion:
Unitarian
Ancestry:
English
Occupation:
Lawyer
Date and place of marriage:
June 19, 1886, Cincinnati, Ohio
Age at marriage:
28 years, 277 days
Years married:
43 years, 262 days
Political party:
Republican
State represented:
Ohio
Term of office:
Mar. 4, 1909-Mar. 3, 1913
Term served:
4 years
Administration:
31st
Congresses:
61st, 62nd
Age at inauguration:
51 years, 170 days
Lived after term:
17 years, 4 days
Occupation after term:
Associate Justice, U.S. Supreme Court
Date of death:
Mar. 8, 1930
Age at death:
72 years, 174 days
Place of death:
Washington, D.C.
Burial place:
Arlington National Cemetery, Arlington, Va.

United States Population: 90,492,000 (1909)

Highlights of Administration: Passage of Postal Savings Act . . . 16th Amendment ratified—collection of taxes on income . . . dollar diplomacy . . . states admitted: New Mexico, Arizona.

Scientific Achievement: 1909, Helicopter—Igor Sikorsky of United States . . . 1911, air conditioning—Willis H. Carrier of United States.

Historical Events: 1909, Peary discovered the North Pole . . . 1910, incorporation of Boy Scouts of America . . . 1911, China's Manchu dynasty overthrown by Sun Yat-sen . . . 1912, Titanic sunk off Newfoundland.

Taft was the sixth president to be born in Ohio and the first President to become Chief Justice of the United States Supreme Court. He was the first who had been a member of a cabinet after the Civil War and the first cabinet member other than a Secretary of State to become President. He was second in scholarship in his Yale class of 1878 which consisted of 132 graduates.

In 1909 Mrs. Taft was instrumental in securing 80 Japanese cherry trees from various nurseries, all that were available at that time, planting them along the banks of the Potomac River. Taft was the first President to pitch a ball to open the baseball season.

President and Mrs. Taft celebrated their silver wedding anniversary at the White House in 1911. He was the first President of 48 states which comprised the Union until 1959. Mrs. Taft was ill during part of her husband's administration and her sister often acted as White House hostess. Taft was the first President to be buried in Arlington National Cemetery, Va.

WOODROW WILSON

28th President

Born:
Dec. 28, 1856
Birthplace:
Staunton, Va.
College attended:
Princeton University, Princeton, N.J.
Date of graduation:
June 18, 1879, Bachelor of Arts
Religion:
Presbyterian
Ancestry:
Scotch-Irish
Occupation:
Teacher, governor
Dates and places of marriages:
June 24, 1885, Savannah, Ga.
Dec. 18, 1915, Washington, D.C.
Ages at marriages:
28 years, 178 days/58 years, 355 days
Years married:
29 years, 43 days/8 years, 47 days
Political party:
Democratic
State represented:
New Jersey
Term of office:
Mar. 4, 1913-Mar. 3, 1921
Term served:
8 years
Administration:
32nd, 33rd
Congresses:
63rd, 64th, 65th, 66th
Age at inauguration:
56 years, 66 days
Lived after term:
2 years, 337 days
Occupation after term:
Lawyer
Date of death:
Feb. 3, 1924
Age at death:
67 years, 37 days
Place of death:
Washington, D.C.
Burial place:
National Cathedral, Washington, D.C.

United States Population: 97,227,000 (1913)

Highlights of Administration: Federal Reserve Act . . . Passage of Clayton Anti-Trust Act . . . signing of Keating-Owen Child Labor Act . . . eight-hour day on railroads established by Adamson Act . . . ratification of 17th Amendment—direct election of Senators . . . ratification of 18th Amendment—prohibition . . . ratification of 19th Amendment—women's suffrage . . . World War I . . . League of Nations.

Scientific Achievement: None.

Historical Events: 1914, assembly-line auto production by Henry Ford . . . 1914, World War 1 started with assassination of Austrian Archduke Ferdinand . . . 1915, beginning of regular transcontinental telephone service in United States . . . 1917, declaration of war against Germany by United States . . . 1917, beginning of Russian Revolution . . . 1918, establishment of socialist dictatorship in Russia by Lenin . . . 1918, World War 1 armistice . . . 1920, first meeting of the League of Nations . . . 1921, first transcontinental airmail flight.

Wilson was the eighth President born in Virginia and the second Democratic President since the Civil War. He was the first to major in history and government at college and the first President who had been president of a major university (Princeton).

He was the fourth to be inaugurated on March 5 (March 4 was a Sunday) and the 11th to be elected from a state other than his native state. Wilson was the third President whose wife died while he was in office, the fifth to remarry and the sixth to marry a widow.

Within about 2 1/2 years, Wilson rose from a man who had never held public office to the President of the United States. The first presidential press conference was held on March 15, 1913, 11 days after Wilson's inauguration.

Wilson's first wife served only 17 months as First Lady of the country, dying in 1914. A daughter took over the functions as White House hostess until December, 1915, when Wilson remarried. When he suffered a paralytic stroke four years later, social activities at the White House were suspended.

WARREN GAMALIEL HARDING

29th President

Born:
Nov. 2, 1865
Birthplace:
Corsica, Ohio
College attended:
Ohio Central College, Iberia, Ohio
Years attended:
1879-1882
Religion:
Baptist
Ancestry:
Scotch-Irish, English
Occupation:
Editor
Date and place of marriage:
July 8, 1891, Marion, Ohio
Age at marriage:
25 years, 248 days
Years married:
32 years, 25 days
Political party:
Republican
State represented:
Ohio
Term of office:
Mar. 4, 1921-Aug. 2, 1923
Term served:
2 years, 151 days
Administration:
34th
Congresses:
67th
Age at inauguration:
55 years, 122 days
Lived after term:
Died in office
Date of death:
Aug. 2, 1923
Age at death:
57 years, 273 days
Place of death:
San Francisco, Calif.
Burial Place:
Hillside Cemetery, Marion, Ohio

United States Population: 105,541,000 (1921)

Highlights of Administration: Creation of U.S. Budget Bureau . . . administrative scandal: "Teapot Dome" . . . limitation on Naval Armaments Treaty.

Scientific Achievement: 1922, radar—Albert H. Taylor and Leo C. Young of United States.

Historical Events: 1922, fourteen Russian states joined to become Union of Soviet Socialist Republics (USSR).

Harding was the seventh President born in Ohio, the sixth elected from that state. He was the second President elected while a senator, the sixth to die in office and the fourth Ohioan to die in office.

Harding was the first newspaper publisher elected to the presidency, the second to marry a woman who had been divorced and the fourth whose father was alive when he was inaugurated.

Presidential election returns were broadcast by radio for the first time by KDKA in Pittsburgh on Nov. 2, 1920, when results of the Harding-Cox election were announced. Accompanied by former President Wilson, Harding rode to the Capitol in an automobile, the first President to ride to his inaugural. Another innovation was the use of an amplifying public address system so that the assembled crowds could hear the proceedings. Harding was the first President to broadcast a speech over radio, doing so in 1922.

He was the first President to visit Alaska and Canada during his term of office. The first cabinet member convicted of a crime was the Secretary of the Interior during the Harding administration. He was found guilty of having received and accepted a bribe of $100,000. He was sentenced to one year in prison and fined $100,000.

WARREN GAMALIEL HARDING

CALVIN COOLIDGE

CALVIN COOLIDGE

30th President

Born:
July 4, 1872
Birthplace:
Plymouth, Vt.
College attended:
Amherst College, Amherst, Mass.
Date of graduation:
June 26, 1895, Bachelor of Arts
Religion:
Congregationalist
Ancestry:
English
Occupation:
Governor, lawyer
Date and place of marriage:
Oct. 4, 1905, Burlington, Vt.
Age at marriage:
33 years, 92 days
Years married:
27 years, 93 days
Political party:
Republican
State represented:
Massachusetts
Term of office:
Aug. 3, 1923—Mar. 3, 1929
(Succeeded upon Harding's death.)
Term served:
5 years, 214 days
Administration:
34th, 35th
Congresses:
68th, 69th, 70th
Age at inauguration:
51 years, 30 days
Lived after term:
3 years, 307 days
Occupation after term:
Writer, columnist
Date of death:
Jan. 5, 1933
Age at death:
60 years, 185 days
Place of death:
Northampton, Mass.
Burial place:
Hillside Cemetery, Plymouth, Vt.

UNITED STATES POPULATION: 111,950,000 (1923)

HIGHLIGHTS OF ADMINISTRATION: Creation of United States Foreign Service . . . granting of citizenship to United States born Indians . . . administrative economy and tax cuts.

SCIENTIFIC ACHIEVEMENT: 1926, television—John L. Baird of Scotland.

HISTORICAL EVENTS: 1926, first flight over North Pole by Richard E. Byrd . . . 1927, transatlantic solo flight by Charles Lindbergh.

Coolidge was the second President born in Vermont and the 12th elected from a state other than his native state. He was the fifth President whose father was alive when he was inaugurated and the first sworn in by his father.

Coolidge was the first whose inaugural ceremonies were broadcast. The first films of presidential candidates were seen by movie spectators in September 1924. Coolidge's 41-minute inaugural speech was broadcast by 25 radio stations and heard by an audience estimated at 22,800,000.

Mrs. Coolidge was not given to much social entertainment. During the Coolidges' residence at the White House, their son, Calvin Jr., died. The President's father also died less than two years later, with the result that White House social functions were greatly curtailed. The first coin bearing the likeness of a living President was the 1926 Sesquicentennial half dollar, the obverse bearing the heads of Presidents Washington and Coolidge and the reverse depicting the Liberty Bell.

CALVIN COOLIDGE

HERBERT CLARK HOOVER

HERBERT CLARK HOOVER

31st President

Born:
Aug. 10, 1874
Birthplace:
West Branch, Iowa
College attended:
Stanford University, Palo Alto, Calif.
Date of graduation:
May 29, 1895, four-year course, Bachelor of Arts
Religious denomination:
Society of Friends (Quaker)
Ancestry:
Swiss-German
Occupation:
Engineer
Date and place of marriage:
Feb. 10, 1899, Monterey, Calif.
Age at marriage:
24 years, 184 days
Years married:
44 years, 331 days
Political party:
Republican
State represented:
California
Term of office:
Mar. 4, 1929-Mar. 3, 1933
Term served:
4 years
Administration:
36th
Congresses:
71st, 72nd
Age at inauguration:
54 years, 206 days
Lived after term:
31 years, 231 days
Occupation after term:
Special reorganization commissions, writing
Date of death:
Oct. 20, 1964
Age at death:
90 years, 71 days
Place of death:
New York, N.Y.
Burial place:
West Branch, Iowa

United States Population: 121,770,000 (1929)

Highlights of Administration: Stock market panic and depression . . . "Star Spangled Banner" adopted as national anthem . . . creation of Reconstruction Finance Corporation . . . ratification of 20th Amendment ("Lame Duck").

Scientific Achievement: None.

Historical Events: 1930, Haile Selassie became emperor of Ethiopia.

Hoover was the first President born in Iowa and the 13th elected from a state other than his native state. He was the first President to have served in a cabinet other than as Secretary of State or War and the last whose term of office ended on March 3. He was the first President born west of the Mississippi River and his wife was the first President's wife born west of the Mississippi. The first asteroid named for an American President was Hooveria.

Hoover established a precedent when he appointed as Chief Justice of the Supreme Court Charles Evans Hughes. It was Hughes' second appointment to the Court, a distinction held by no other person. The first absolute monarch to visit the United States was King Prajadhipok of Siam.

Hoover's wife had numerous personal friends in the city when they moved into the White House and as a result social functions were more friendly than formal. He was one of the most honored of American Presidents receiving over 50 honorary degrees from American universities, over 25 honorary degrees from foreign universities, the freedom of more than a dozen cities, and over 70 medals and awards in addition to about 100 miscellaneous honors.

HERBERT CLARK HOOVER

FRANKLIN DELANO ROOSEVELT

FRANKLIN DELANO ROOSEVELT

32nd President

Born:
Jan. 30, 1882
Birthplace:
Hyde Park, N.Y.
College attended:
Harvard College, Cambridge, Mass.
Date of graduation:
June 24, 1903, four-year course, Bachelor of Arts
Religion:
Episcopalian
Ancestry:
Dutch
Occupation:
Governor, lawyer
Date and place of marriage:
Mar. 17, 1905, New York, N.Y.
Age at marriage:
23 years, 46 days
Years married:
40 years, 26 days
Political party:
Democratic
State represented:
New York
Term of office:
Mar. 4, 1933-Apr. 12, 1945
Term served:
12 years, 39 days
Administration:
37th, 38th, 39th, 40th
Congresses:
73rd, 74th, 75th, 76th, 77th, 78th, 79th
Age at inauguration:
51 years, 33 days
Lived after term:
Died in office
Date of death:
Apr. 12, 1945
Age at death:
63 years, 72 days
Place of death:
Warm Springs, Ga.
Burial place:
Family plot, Hyde Park, N.Y.

United States Population: 125,579,000 (1923)

Highlights of Administration: New Deal recovery reform . . . extensive public works programs . . . Civilian Conservation Corps . . . Agricultural Adjustment Act . . . National Industrial Recovery Act . . . Social Security Act . . . Wagner Labor Act . . . Federal Housing Act . . . Works Progress Administration . . . Tennessee Valley Authority . . . Federal Housing Administration . . . World War II . . . only President elected for more than two terms.

Scientific Achievement: 1937, nylon—Wallace H. Carothers of United States . . . 1937, electronic computer—Howard Aiken of United States . . . 1937, jet engine—Sir Frank Whittle of England.

Historical Events: 1933, Wiley Post—solo world flight . . . 1933, United States and USSR establish diplomatic relations . . . 1934, Adolf Hitler became dictator of Germany . . . 1936, King George VI took throne of England upon abdication of Edward VIII . . . 1939, end of Spanish Civil War announced by Spain's Generalissimo Franco . . . 1939, World War II started with invasion of Poland by Germany . . . 1941, Japanese attack on Pearl Harbor, United States entry into World War II.

Roosevelt was the fourth President born in New York and the seventh to die in office. He was the eighth whose mother was alive when he was inaugurated and the first President whose mother could have voted for him for the presidency. He was the third Democratic President since the Civil War. He was the first elected to a third term (and also a fourth term).

An attempt on Roosevelt's life was made in Miami, Fla. on Feb. 15, 1933, but the shot missed and instead killed the mayor of Chicago. Roosevelt also appointed the first woman to a cabinet post, Frances Perkins as Secretary of Labor. He also appointed the first woman to represent the United States as a minister to a foreign country.

Roosevelt gave the 1936 Republican candidate one of the worst defeats in presidential elections, beating Alfred H. Landon by carrying all 48 states except Maine and Vermont and receiving 523 electoral votes out of 531.

FRANKLIN DELANO ROOSEVELT

HARRY S. TRUMAN

HARRY S. TRUMAN
33rd President

Born:
May 8, 1884
Birthplace:
Lamar, Mo.
College attended:
None
Religion:
Baptist
Ancestry:
English-Scotch-Irish
Occupation:
Farmer, haberdasher, judge, senator, Vice President
Date of marriage:
June 28, 1919, Independence, Mo.
Age at marriage:
35 years, 51 days
Years married:
53 years, 181 days
Political party:
Democratic
State represented:
Missouri
Term of office:
Apr. 12, 1945—Jan. 20, 1953
(Succeeded upon Roosevelt's death.)
Term served:
7 years, 283 days
Administration:
40th, 41st
Congresses:
79th, 80th, 81st, 82nd
Age at inauguration:
60 years, 339 days
Lived after term:
19 years, 340 days
Occupation after term:
Retired, writer
Date of death:
Dec. 26, 1972
Age at death:
88 years, 232 days
Place of death:
Kansas City, Mo.
Burial place:
Independence, Mo.

United States Population: 132,481,000 (1945)

Highlights of Administration: United Nations charter signed . . . World War II ended . . . Taft-Hartley Act: labor-management . . . McCarran-Walter Immigration bill . . . creation of North Atlantic Treaty Alliance . . . Marshall Plan for European recovery . . . Truman Doctrine for foreign aid . . . Korean War . . . 22nd Amendment—Presidents limited to two terms.

Scientific Achievement: 1945, atomic bomb (first detonated)—International team of scientists, United States.

Historical Events: 1945, V-E Day . . . 1945, United States atomic bomb dropped in Japan . . . 1945, World War II ended with surrender of Japan . . . 1947, independence from Britain for India and Pakistan . . . 1948, assassination of Mahatma Gandhi . . . 1951, first transcontinental TV broadcast.

Truman was the first President born in Missouri, the ninth whose mother was alive when he was inaugurated and the fourth Democratic President since the Civil War.

The initial "S" in Truman's name has no special significance and is not an abbreviation of any name. It is said to have been chosen by his parents to avoid a display of favoritism since his maternal and paternal grandfather's names were Solomon Young and Anderson Shippe Truman, respectively.

He was the first President to travel in a submarine, doing so in 1946. The first Presidential address telecast from the White House was delivered by Truman on Oct. 5, 1947.

As assassination attempt was made on Truman's life on Nov. 1, 1950 by two Puerto Rican nationalists, who tried to shoot their way into Blair House, the Truman's private residence. Truman was the first President to officially receive a woman ambassador from a foreign country, receiving the ambassador of India.

Mrs. Truman, in contrast to her predecessor, was very retiring and endeavored to keep out of the public eye as much as possible. She was well-known to an intimate group of Washington friends. The Truman's daughter, Margaret, made frequent appearances as a concert singer and television performer.

HARRY S. TRUMAN

DWIGHT DAVID EISENHOWER

DWIGHT DAVID EISENHOWER
34th President

Born:
Oct. 14, 1890 (Given name—David Dwight)
Birthplace:
Denison, Tex.
College attended:
United States Military Academy, West Point, N.Y.
Date of graduation:
June 12, 1915, four-year course
Religion:
Presbyterian
Ancestry:
Swiss-German
Occupation:
Army officer
Date and place of marriage:
July 1, 1916, Denver, Colo.
Age at marriage:
25 years, 260 days
Years married:
52 years, 270 days
Political party:
Republican
State represented:
New York
Term of office:
Jan. 20, 1953-Jan. 20, 1961
Term served:
8 years
Administration:
42nd, 43rd
Congresses:
83rd, 84th, 85th, 86th
Age at inauguration:
62 years, 98 days
Lived after term:
8 years, 67 days
Occupation after term:
Retired, author
Date of death:
Mar. 28, 1969
Age at death:
79 years, 165 days
Place of death:
Washington, D.C.
Burial place:
Abilene, Kan.

United States Population: 158,434,000 (1953)

Highlights of Administration: End of Korean War . . . Southeast Asia Treaty Organization . . . creation of Department of Health, Education and Welfare . . . St. Lawrence Seaway opened . . . Civil Rights Commission . . . NASA . . . McCarthy hearings . . . Eisenhower Doctrine . . . states admitted: Alaska, Hawaii.

Scientific Achievement: 1953, polio vaccine—Dr. Jonas Salk of United States . . . 1960, Laser—Charles H. Townes of United States.

Historical Events: 1953, end of Korean War . . . 1957, Sputnik 1 launched by Soviet Union . . . 1959, Fidel Castro assumed leadership of Cuba . . . 1960, Belgian Congo independent.

Eisenhower was the first President born in Texas, the 14th elected from a state other than his native state and the first to serve a constitutionally limited president term. He was the first Republican in the twentieth century to win two successive presidential elections, the first President of 49 (and later 50) states, and the first to serve with three congresses in which both chambers were controlled by an opposing political party.

Eisenhower appointed grandsons to positions held by their grandfathers (John Foster Dulles as Secretary of State, and John Marshall Harlan as Associate Justice of the Supreme Court).

He held the first presidential news conference to be recorded on both newsreel and television in January, 1955. The greatest popular vote in the history of the United States was recorded on Nov. 6, 1956, when over 35,581,000 cast their vote for Eisenhower, or over 57 percent, compared to Adlai Stevenson's 26,031,000 votes, or almost 42 percent, for a total of about 62,000,000 popular votes. Eisenhower was the first President to submerge in an atomic-powered submarine.

Mrs. Eisenhower was one of the most reserved, dignified and unassuming First Lady's in history because before her husband's administration, as an army wife for 37 years, she grew accustomed to meeting groups of influential people.

JOHN FITZGERALD KENNEDY

35th President

Born:
May 29, 1917
Birthplace:
Brookline, Mass.
College attended:
Harvard College, Cambridge, Mass.
Date of graduation:
June 21, 1940, B.S. cum laude
Religion:
Roman Catholic
Ancestry:
Irish
Occupation:
Author, congressman, senator
Date and place of marriage:
Sept. 12, 1953, Newport, R.I.
Age at marriage:
36 years, 106 days
Years married:
10 years, 71 days
Political party:
Democratic
State represented:
Massachusetts
Term of office:
Jan. 20, 1961-Nov. 22, 1963
Term served:
2 years, 306 days
Administration:
44th
Congresses:
87th, 88th
Age at inauguration:
43 years, 236 days
Lived after term:
Died in office
Date of death:
Nov. 22, 1963
Age at death:
46 years, 177 days
Place of death:
Dallas, Tex.
Burial place:
Arlington National Cemetery, Va.

United States Population: 183,650,000 (1961)

Highlights of Administration: Bay of Pigs invasion of Cuba . . . Peace Corps Act . . . legislation for federal aid to education . . . beginning of Alliance for Progress . . . civil rights legislation . . . Cuban missile confrontation . . . nuclear test ban treaty limitation.

Scientific Achievement: None.

Historical Events: 1961, Russian Yuri Gagarin first man to orbit earth . . . 1962, France and Algeria hostilities ended after seven year war . . . 1962, first United States astronaut to orbit earth—John Glenn . . . 1963, beginning of Federation of Malaysia.

Kennedy was the first President born in the twentieth century, the first Roman Catholic and the first to be inaugurated on the new east front of the United States Capitol. He was also the first President whose parents survived him, the first whose inaugural was celebrated by five inaugural balls, the first whose inaugural was shown on color television and the first who served in the navy. Kennedy was the second President to be buried in Arlington National Cemetery, Va., the fourth to be assassinated and the eighth to die in office.

The first presidential candidate debate series on television involved Kennedy and Republican Richard M. Nixon. Kennedy survived the closest popular vote in United States history when on Nov. 8, 1960, he received 34,227,096 votes (49.71 percent) to Nixon's 34,107,646 votes (49.55 percent).

He was the youngest presidential nominee elected and the youngest man elected to office but not the youngest President (Theodore Roosevelt holds that distinction).

Kennedy was assassinated in Dallas, Texas on Nov. 22, 1963, while riding in an automobile procession. His accused assassin was Lee Harvey Oswald of Dallas, who, in turn, was shot and killed two days after Kennedy died, by Jack Ruby of Dallas, in the Dallas Police Station.

Kennedy's wife, Jacqueline, was the first incumbent President's wife to be received in private audience by the Pope (March 1962).

JOHN FITZGERALD KENNEDY

LYNDON BAINES JOHNSON

LYNDON BAINES JOHNSON
36th President

Born:
Aug. 27, 1908
Birthplace:
Near Stonewall, Tex.
College attended:
Southwest Texas State College, San Marcos
Date of graduation:
Aug. 19, 1930, B.S. degree
Religion:
Disciples of Christ (International Convention of Christian Churches)
Ancestry:
British
Occupation:
Senator, rancher
Date and place of marriage:
Nov. 17, 1934, San Antonio, Tex.
Age at marriage:
26 years, 82 days
Years married:
39 years, 66 days
Political party:
Democratic
State represented:
Texas
Terms of office:
Nov. 22, 1963—Jan. 20, 1969 (Succeeded upon Kennedy's death.)
Term served:
5 years, 59 days
Administration:
44th, 45th
Congresses:
88th, 89th, 90th
Age at inauguration:
55 years, 87 days
Lived after term:
4 years, 2 days
Date of death:
Jan. 22, 1973
Age at death:
65 years, 148 days
Place of death:
San Antonio, Tex.
Burial place:
Johnson City, Tex.

United States Population: 189,042,000 (1963 estimated)

Highlights of Administration: Medicare health plan . . . increased Social Security benefits . . . legislated aid to education . . . creation of Department of Housing and Urban Development . . . escalation of Vietnam . . . Dominican Republic intervention . . . ratification of 24th Amendment—poll taxes banned in federal elections.

Scientific Achievement: 1965, commercial communications satellite—United States scientists . . . 1967, first human heart transplant by Dr. Christian Barnard, South Africa.

Historical Events: 1967, evidence dating man's origin 2.5 million years discovered by Harvard archaeologists in Kenya.

Johnson established many "firsts" as President. Included were: the first from a southern state since Zachary Taylor; to ride in an armored automobile at his inauguration; to take the oath of office in an airplane; to be sworn in by a woman; who took his oath on a Bible held by his wife; to be inaugurated in a business suit. Also, the first to witness the assassination of the President whom he succeeded in office; Democratic president to carry Vermont and the first to carry Maine since 1912; and to have an inaugural parade in which the Air Force paraded.

Johnson was the second born in Texas and the second named Johnson to succeed to the presidency on the death of an incumbent. He was the third Vice President named Johnson, the fourth to become President as the result of an assassination and the eighth to become President as the result of the death of his predecessor. He was the first President, who, with his wife, received honorary degrees simultaneously (University of Texas, May 1964).

Two new cabinet posts were created during his administration: Department of Housing and Urban Development and Department of Transportation. Johnson was the first President to confer in the United States with a Pope (Pope Paul VI in New York City, October 1965).

LYNDON BAINES JOHNSON

RICHARD
MILHOUS NIXON

RICHARD MILHOUS NIXON

37th President

Born:
Jan. 9, 1913
Birthplace:
Yorba Linda, Calif.
Colleges attended:
Whittier College (B.A., 1934);
Duke University Law School
(LL.B., 1937)
Religion:
Quaker
Ancestry:
English, Scotch-Irish
Occupations:
Lawyer, public official
Date and place of marriage:
June 21, 1940,
to Thelma Patricia Ryan
in Riverside, Calif.
Age at marriage:
27 years, 163 days
Political Party:
Republican
State Represented:
New York
Military service:
United States Navy (1942-1946)
Principal writing:
Six Crises (1962)
Term of office:
Jan. 20, 1969—Aug. 9, 1974
Terms served:
1 1/2 terms
Administration:
46th, 47th
Congresses:
91st, 92nd, 93rd
Age at inauguration:
56 years, 11 days

United States Population: 195,000,000 (1969 estimated)

Highlights of Administration: Policy of troop withdrawal from Vietnam

Scientific Achievement: None.

Historical Events: 1969, United States Astronauts Neil Armstrong and Edwin Aldrin Jr. took first moon walk.

Nixon entered the White House in 1969 while the nation was deeply divided over the war in Vietnam. He ended United States involvement in that conflict after four years of tedious negotiations. Striving to achieve a "generation of peace," the President improved relations with the Soviet Union and the People's Republic of China, the two most powerful Communist nations. To advance this effort, he made dramatic visits to Peking and Moscow.

Although he was elected to the presidency by a narrow margin in 1968, he won a sweeping landslide in 1972, carrying 49 of 50 states.

However, his standing soon fell as details of the Watergate affair became known in judicial proceedings and legislative hearings. The break-in at the Democratic National Committee headquarters in Washington, D.C. was one of a number of illegal or unethical activities relating to Nixon's reelection campaign. Several dozen public officials, campaign workers and financial contributors were implicated. Under pressure of possible impeachment, Nixon became the first President to resign from office.

Before becoming President, Nixon served in the United States House of Representatives, the United States Senate and as Vice President. An articulate spokesman for the Republican party, he was named to the GOP national ticket five times, more than anyone else.

He had inherited a country at war and at times beset with domestic unrest and violence but his inauguration theme of unity and public trust soon was destroyed by the scandal of the Watergate affair.

RICHARD MILHOUS NIXON

GERALD R. FORD

GERALD R. FORD

38th President

Born:
July 14, 1913
Birthplace:
Omaha, Nebr.
Colleges attended:
University of Michigan (B.A., 1935); Yale University Law School (LL.B., 1941)
Religion:
Episcopalian
Date of marriage:
Oct. 15, 1948
Political party:
Republican
State represented:
Michigan
Term of office:
Aug. 9, 1974—
Administration:
48th
Congresses:
93rd, 94th
Age at inauguration:
61 years
Military service:
United States Navy (1942-1946)

HIGHLIGHTS OF ADMINISTRATION: None.

SCIENTIFIC ACHIEVEMENT: None.

HISTORICAL EVENTS: None.

Ford was an American political leader, who in 1973 was nominated by Nixon to be Vice President of the United States after Spiro Agnew resigned. He served in the United States Navy for 47 months during World War II, serving aboard an aircraft carrier for two years. After his discharge as a lieutenant commander in 1946 he resumed the practice of law.

He was elected to the House of Representatives in 1948 and reelected every two years through 1972, serving 25 years in the House. In 1963, he was named to the Presidential Commission investigating the assassination of President Kennedy. He was the co-author of "Portrait of the Assassin" (1965) and was permanent chairman of the 1968 and 1972 Republican National Conventions.

Ford visited the People's Republic of China in late June and early July 1972 on behalf of President Nixon. He was minority leader of the 89th, 90th, 91st, 92nd and 1st Session of the 93rd Congresses. He was nominated Vice President on Oct. 12, 1973. He was confirmed Dec. 6, 1973, succeeding to the presidency Aug. 9, 1974 following the resignation of President Nixon.

Ford advocated economy in government and criticized the "Great Society" programs proposed by former President Johnson. Ford favored defense and space programs, and as an internationalist he advocated a major world role for the United States. He was a close friend of Nixon for many years, and strongly supported Nixon's policies in Indochina and in domestic affairs.

GERALD R. FORD